PENCIL
BROADSIDES

FIFTH AVENUE, NEW YORK

PENCIL
BROADSIDES

A Manual of Broad Stroke Technique

THEODORE KAUTZKY

VAN NOSTRAND REINHOLD COMPANY

NEW YORK   CINCINNATI   TORONTO   LONDON   MELBOURNE

Van Nostrand Reinhold Company Regional Offices:
New York Cincinnati Chicago Millbrae Dallas

Van Nostrand Reinhold Company International Offices:
London Toronto Melbourne

Published by Van Nostrand Reinhold Company
450 West 33rd Street, New York, N.Y. 10001

Published simultaneously in Canada by
Van Nostrand Reinhold Ltd.

16 15 14 13 12 11 10 9 8

TABLE OF CONTENTS

PART I   BROAD STROKE TECHNIQUE

PART II   PORTFOLIO OF BROAD STROKE DRAWINGS

PART I

BROAD STROKE TECHNIQUE

LESSON 1—FUNDAMENTAL STROKES

In preparing the series of lessons in pencil drawing that begins here, there is no wish to add unnecessarily to the already substantial list of excellent general books on this subject now available. It is my purpose to discuss only one particular technique — a technique that so far as I know has not been completely explored elsewhere. For want of a better name, it may be called "broad stroke pencil drawing." Used with intelligence and artistic sense it is capable of yielding crisp, sparkling, and powerfully expressive results.

Proficiency with this technique may be reached in proportion to the degree of control that is acquired over a few simple but fundamental strokes that will be described hereafter. These can be mastered by anyone who is willing to practice them diligently. For complete success they *must* be mastered; so don't be tempted to regard them as too elementary for you.

For practice you will need paper, pencils, and means to keep the latter properly sharp. As you develop skill you will develop preferences as to materials, but at this stage it will be well to select kid-finish Bristol or some paper of similar surface and a good quality drawing pencil of 2B grade. For deeper blacks you may sometimes need a 4B but no others are really necessary. A sharp knife and a sandpaper block will complete your equipment. The sandpaper block is just as important as the pencil. Don't forget it.

After the wood of the pencil has been whittled away to expose about a quarter of an inch of cylindrical lead, the lead is rubbed at an angle on the sandpaper to produce a flat wedge point as at 2. or 3. of the accompanying plate. The broad strokes are to be made with the flat side of this wedge held evenly against the paper. The width of strokes will depend on the angle at which the point is sharpened. Note that the surface of the lead held against the paper will be oval-shaped, since it is a section cut by a plane intersecting a cylinder. This oval shape allows more flexibility in producing different types of stroke than could be had with a square lead.

Now with this flat surface of the pencil point held full against the paper, a stroke can be drawn which begins and ends cleanly, is of uniform width, and has the same value throughout. If the pencil is slightly tilted, however, toward its point, as at 4., or away from it, as at 5., the same pressure will yield a stroke accented and sharp along one edge and fading out along the other. By rocking the pencil, alternately back and forth during the stroke, the result shown at 6. is secured. Thin lines for outline or accents (similar to those made by a conical point, as at 1.) may be produced by holding the wedge pointed pencil upright.

The broad strokes, incidentally, should all be made at the same steady speed, not too fast nor yet too slow. They should also be made by moving the arm rather than the fingers.

Rolling the pencil very slightly, either away from or towards you, and holding it that way during a stroke, will reduce the area of lead in contact with the paper and so with the same pressure will yield a stroke of darker value.

After you have practiced these single strokes of various types for a while, try to combine them to produce flat and graded wash effects as at A. In these, the strokes are laid side by side, touching each other but not overlapping, so that individual strokes merge with their neighbors. Try to keep the beginning and end of each stroke clean and square with the rest so that when you are done the area you have covered will be definitely rectangular. You will learn to slide the pencil very slightly across the stroke at its beginning and end to get this clean termination without increasing the pressure.

Sometimes in covering an area it is desirable to break the monotony of parallel strokes by introducing some diagonal strokes which may be thought of as following the direction of light. Practice this as shown at B. in both flat and graded wash effects.

The third exercise in covering areas should be done with a large number of short strokes curving in different directions and combining, as at C., to give either flat or graded values. Acquire all the skill you can at doing these "simple" exercises so that you will be ready in the next lesson to tackle the indication of stonework.

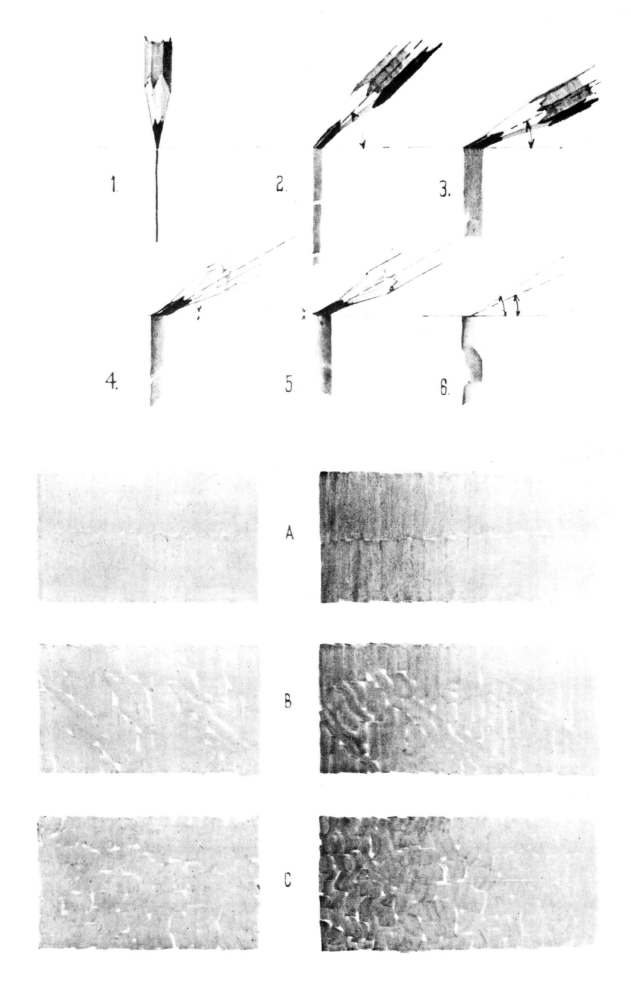

LESSON 2—INDICATING STONEWORK

Having practiced diligently (I hope) the fundamental strokes described in the first lesson, and possessing as a result a reasonable degree of control over the pencil, you are ready to start on the indication of various textures. This lesson has to do with stonework.

While it is possible for you to begin right here, using as reference the examples shown opposite , it would be a wise thing to wait, before you draw, long enough to go outdoors and look at some actual stone walls. There are many things about them that you can observe with profit. Notice the variations in size and color and value of the individual stones in a section of rubble or random ashlar. See how a good mason composes them to achieve variety and texture and how he avoids monotony. See how the light falls differently upon each one and how the shadows and highlights arrange themselves in accordance with the roughness or smoothness of the work. Take note of the effect of reflected light from nearby surfaces or from the ground. The more closely you observe these things, the better able will you be to draw a convincing picture. Even if you are already familiar with stonework, you can always benefit by looking again.

Now come back to your drawing board and see that your sandpaper block is at hand and your pencil is sharpened properly. You are going to try to do what the good mason does — only you will do it on paper.

First you will have to sketch very lightly the pattern of the wall. As you do this, keep in mind the desirability of laying the stones horizontal, mixing the sizes to make a pleasant variety, breaking the joints to get a good bond. Bigger stones are good at corners to give them strength; smaller stones fill in among the irregular spaces between the big ones. If you are drawing a rough wall, avoid the monotony of pattern that would be caused by repeating stones of the same size or shape at regular intervals.

Decide where you want to focus the attention by giving your wall the greatest contrast with its surroundings. Begin there to put in the darkest values, shading individual stones cleanly with parallel strokes of the required weight. Do some stones with vertical strokes; a few with horizontal for variety's sake. Or vice-versa. Occasionally, as you proceed from dark toward light, break the pattern with some diagonal strokes as you did in the last lesson at "B." Keep the edges of stones clean-cut by accenting the beginning and end of strokes slightly as already described. This applies particularly to the edges that silhouette against the sky or lighter areas.

Put in a few shadows along the bottom edges of occasional stones, watching the whole effect all the while to avoid spottiness. Leave clean white areas between stones to count partly as mortar joints, partly as highlights along top edges, but avoid monotony in this also by letting some strokes pass through from stone to stone.

By working from dark toward light, you can keep the entire area under better control and you will learn with experience that there comes a point where it is well to stop with some of the stones left white. The white areas give sparkle to the final result and are in accord with nature, where sunlight is almost totally reflected from surfaces upon which it falls at just the proper angle. Even in shadows it is well to leave a little white paper to show through here and there to express reflected light and break up otherwise uninteresting areas.

The same general method is applicable to any type of stonework. As the wall becomes smoother, individual stones are drawn with less gradation and the shadows under them become less pronounced. The same is true of the highlights. There is still, however, gradation from dark to light in the whole picture and individual stones are not all in the same value. The diagonal strokes are still used to give variety and to suggest the direction of falling light. Stiffness can be avoided without interfering with the general effect of accurate jointing and dressing, as may be seen in the example at the bottom of the accompanying sheet.

Three types of stonework only are shown. In them, nevertheless, you can find the principles by which to indicate any of the many varieties of texture you will see in buildings, stone fences, etc., as you travel about. Try many of them.

LESSON 3—INDICATING BRICKWORK

This lesson turns to the problem of indicating brickwork at both small and large scale. The illustrations show two examples which in scale are approximately what you might encounter in an architectural perspective rendering, but the principles back of their execution extend to cover any reasonable scale.

The same suggestion I previously made with regard to stone textures applies to brickwork. That is, you can to advantage go out before you begin to draw and look closely at a number of brick walls, making a mental note of the things that give them their character both when seen at a little distance and near at hand. Differences in color of individual bricks, shadows in the mortar joints, the type of bond, and the thickness of joints become of more importance as the scale increases. At the smaller scale, these things cannot be shown in detail but it is important to know that they exist if you want to be intelligent about suggesting them with your pencil.

At the smaller scale, one of the important things to look out for is the perspective direction of the brick courses. The example shown is seen almost in direct elevation and there was not much chance of going astray. When the surface of the wall is viewed at more of an angle, however, watch carefully to keep the direction of courses correct as you work down the wall.

Assuming that you have now laid out your drawing lightly, we will start to render it. Decide in your mind, if possible, how you are going to dispose your values to get an interesting composition with dark against light and light against dark and a sparkling play of sunshine and shadow. Begin to put in the darkest values. For the shadows, use broad diagonal strokes, making them not too dense and allowing occasional spots of white to break up any monotonous areas.

Now begin at the top of the brick surface to render the brick itself. In doing this, avoid monotony by varying the length of strokes from course to course. Do not indicate each separate brick but occasionally use a short stroke among the longer ones. Break the horizontal strokes by introducing diagonal lines once in a while and sometimes cover an irregular area with a series of short diagonals, keeping the value the same as adjacent brick courses. The wall in general should grade from dark at the top to light at the bottom. As you work down, you can leave more whites to show through between courses, but everywhere avoid monotony or regularity. To suggest weathering, use some vertical shading, particularly near the top where it would occur in nature. These vertical strokes can be put in either as you render or later, on top of earlier strokes. You can also put in some dark bricks here and there, but don't overdo it.

When you finish, if you are successful, you will have indicated a brick surface that has a convincing texture, that is full of interest, that provides contrasts where you want them, and that suggests shadows falling from nearby trees.

Turning to larger scale, the things you have now learned can be applied with more exactitude, but no less freedom. In the piece of wall shown at the bottom of the accompanying plate, the individual bricks show up more clearly but the surface is well broken up with diagonal strokes and areas shaded to the appropriate values. Here, the individual bricks appear as single strokes made with a properly sharpened pencil. They vary in value as the bricks themselves vary in color. Shadows have been indicated sharply under some of them and the mortar joints are left white in many places, taking care however to distribute the sparkling whites irregularly. If you practice copying this drawing and then apply what you learn to examples of your own invention you will acquire freedom and command as you go along.

If you do not succeed in producing a satisfactory result, it may be that you need to refer back to Lesson 1 and do some more practice of individual strokes. It may be because you are not keeping your pencil properly sharpened. Or it may be that you are not keeping in mind at all times that monotony must be avoided through variety of strokes, contrasting values, and opposition of forms. Only by exercising constant control over your whole composition, seeing it broadly while you are drawing in detail, can you produce a completely artistic result. But keep on trying.

13

LESSON 4—A FEW WOOD TEXTURES

The sketches shown in Lesson 4 illustrate the handling of a sufficient variety of wood textural problems to keep you busy practicing for a while. The first example, at the top, includes weathered shingle roof and shingled walls painted, let us assume, white.

Begin, as usual, after laying out the sketch lightly, by putting in the darkest areas. The principal one of these, in the subject chosen, is the roof. In indicating this there are three things to be shown — the tone of the roof itself, weathered or perhaps stained to a rather dark value; the contrasting tone of the end grain showing along the butts, which resolves itself into a series of parallel but slightly irregular and discontinuous lines; and the still darker shadows falling across the roof, cast by the chimney and nearby trees. This analysis suggests three principal directions for your strokes — broad strokes paralleling the grain of the shingles to cover the general tone, narrower strokes along the lines of butts, and broad strokes following the direction of falling light. Start by laying in the general value of the roof area with long and short broad strokes. The shortest ones will be determined by the height of a single course or row of shingles.

Since the tree and chimney shadows will be the darkest values, it will be economical of effort to put them in early in the game, using strokes whose direction follows the direction of light.

Now, using your pencil with a narrower surface in contact with the paper, put in some of the irregular parallel lines which represent the butts of the shingles. As you will observe by looking at a shingle roof, these strokes should not be straight and stiff and they should vary in thickness slightly from point to point. They should not extend over the entire surface of the roof, but only enough to give a realistic effect.

Indication of the dark accenting shadows of the doorway and the window lights can be done at this point or even before, the idea being to keep everything in proper relation to the whole as you proceed. The door itself, as an important part of the center of interest, should be given its proper value with carefully controlled broad strokes, leaving highlights along the edges of the rails and stiles. The dark foliage and the tree trunks can be indicated at this stage also. Do this rather carefully and deliberately, taking care to silhouette the corner of the house with a slightly saw-tooth effect to express the overlapping rows of shingles.

The same procedure as for the roof may be followed for the walls except that here the shadows, which supply the principal means of distributing interest, should definitely come first. Draw them in with broad gray strokes, with some feeling for reality and also with some understanding of how they will modify contrasts. The strongest contrasts should come near the center of interest. Therefore, where you have a dark value which, if silhouetted against a light area, would draw the eye powerfully to that point, you reduce the contrast as needed to keep the interest where it belongs. The right-hand end of the roof, if set against the white sky, would be too prominent. For this reason, I have put in some gray foliage and tree trunks to soften the contrast. (This foliage, incidentally, extended upward, is useful in defining the corner of the chimney.) You can find other places illustrating the principle.

Having cast the necessary shadows which help to keep your composition in hand, you can now indicate the shingle courses by rows of short, broad, vertical strokes for the shingles themselves and narrow horizontal strokes for the shadows at the butts.

Passing now to the sketch in which rough siding is represented, there is little to be said that will not be evident upon thoughtful inspection of the drawing. The principal area is all put in with broad, vertical strokes and the edges of the siding with their shadows are more irregular in spacing and direction than those of shingles.

Having gone so far, the indication of the clapboarded house should present no difficult problem. Work from dark to light, as always, and put your foliage shadows in before accenting the shadows under each row of clapboards. Restrain yourself as you work along, always trying to determine, in time, the point at which to stop.

LESSON 5—DRAWING THE PINE TREE

For the next few lessons I am going to discuss the drawing of different types of trees. Many people who can make a satisfactory representation of an architectural subject seem satisfied if they can suggest its setting by means of nondescript or stereotyped trees and shrubbery. I feel very strongly that it is worth while to learn to draw trees that really look like trees and that can be identified as oak or birch or pine or some other definite species.

The first essential is an understanding of the tree structure. You should, by observation of actual specimens, fix in your mind the characteristics of each kind of tree, the relation between its various parts, between trunk and branch, twig and leaf, and so on. Realize that it is a three-dimensional object which can be thought of in terms of plan as well as elevation. Light falling upon it will strike full against some of the foliage masses while others will be in shade or in shadow. Some of the branches extend towards the observer, some away, and some to either side of the trunk. These things seem elementary, but I have seen so many drawings which show a disregard for the simplest facts of tree structure that it is worth while to point them out. By keeping them in mind you will avoid drawing the hard, formless silhouettes or feather-dustery monstrosities that so unnecessarily mar the work of many amateur sketchers.

At 1, 2, and 3 on the accompanying plate, I have diagrammatically shown a section of weatherbeaten pine tree with four branches. In plan, the branches, each bearing an irregular mass of needles, radiate in four directions from the trunk, filling out a rough circle. In elevation, the four branches appear at different levels, extending out and down from the trunk and terminating in up-curving, finger-like twigs supporting the foliage. With light falling from the left and above and striking the tops of these foliage masses, the sides you are looking at would be about as shown, generally dark in value with a suggestion of sunlight along the top surfaces. Where the foliage is in back of the trunk, the trunk will appear light against the dark needles beyond. Where the branch comes

out towards the light, its foliage casts a shadow on the trunk below. So much for this analysis, the application of which will become clear as you proceed with a finished sketch, either a copy of this plate or composed according to fancy.

In young pines the branches start from the trunk at an upward angle. As the tree grows older and the foliage masses become heavier and extend farther out from the trunk, the branches are weighted down into a graceful, elongated S-curve. At first there are possibly six or more radiating branches at each level. In the tree's life, however, branches break off or are cut off until when it becomes old it is likely to be irregular and picturesque like the ones shown here. One can take liberties in arranging the foliage of this sort of trees to conform with the requirements of a picture, without much danger of departing from reality, provided the general rules of structure are not violated.

In rendering the foliage of these trees, I have used short broad strokes for the most part, with narrower radiating strokes, made with the narrower side of the broad-pointed pencil, around the edges of each mass. This treatment makes a clean, sharp silhouette against the sky, which is left white, and suggests, without being too literal, the needles which make up the foliage.

While the general tone of evergreen foliage is dark, you will note that I have made the portions receiving the light from the sky distinctly lighter than those portions in shade, away from the light, or in shadow. You will also observe, in some places, allowance for light reflected up from the ground into the shaded areas.

The branches and twigs either silhouette dark against the sky or light against dark foliage behind them. Since the bark is comparatively smooth, it may be rendered with broad strokes laid with a little texture. Where, for purposes of composition, a light area of foliage needs to be suggested, as in the branches vignetting at the upper right of our little picture, it is convincing enough to put in the radiating zig-zag strokes around the edges. The eye is satisfied because the more completely rendered masses of the other trees have told the story by suggestion.

LESSON 6—DRAWING THE OAK TREE

In discussing the correct drawing of trees, I wish to make it clear that my interest in distinguishing between species is not that of a scientific botanist, nor do I pretend to any botanical exactitude in my drawings. I regard the trees I draw from the point of view of an artist who wishes to be convincingly truthful and who loves trees for the sake of their interesting forms, the rhythmic lines of their structural elements, and the play of light and shade and color through their foliage masses.

The oak, which is the subject of this lesson, offers marked contrast to the pine, which was treated in the last plate. Characterized by great strength of structure, its heavy trunk and gnarled twisting limbs support a broad, heavily-leafed crown. I have chosen to illustrate here a rather symmetrical example—one whose spreading branches extend about as far horizontally as the tree reaches vertically. The general shape of the whole might be roughly contained within a great sphere and if you keep this thought in mind you will feel the form as you render it.

As usual we begin by drawing lightly the structure of the tree, its thick sturdy trunk tapering up from the ground, dividing itself into several principal limbs which throw off heavy branches as they ascend with many undulations towards the top, reducing gradually their diameters until they divide into smaller branches and twigs which carry the leaves. From the main limbs extend occasional turnings, twisting minor limbs, struggling their way towards the enclosing periphery, crossing and recrossing each other as they go and casting their shadows on their neighbors. We also sketch in the foliage masses and suggest lightly the shades and shadows preparatory to their final expression with broad strokes. The light in this case is falling from the left, above and behind the observer. Keeping in mind the ball-like general mass, you will be able to determine where the lighter and darker portions will occur and cast the foliage shadows on branch, trunk, and ground. When you have drawn your tree something like the little diagram at the top of the plate, only much lighter, you will be ready to go ahead, with essentials established.

Start with the darkest areas, putting them in with broad strokes, rather short to suggest leafage and remembering to silhouette the edges of each mass sharply against the sky with appropriately irregular profile. Heavy limbs in shadow may be shown by strokes running either lengthwise or crosswise. The short strokes running crosswise give a slight vibration to the profiles of the limbs, which is in accord with the roughness of the bark and at the same time helps to suggest the play of reflected light. Longitudinal strokes may be used for the smaller branches and for limbs which catch the light on one side. Remember that limbs and branches passing in front of dark areas should be left white where they catch the light or gray where you want them to show up in shadow. Against the light sky they should show up as clean dark strokes, their values varying with light conditions. It is these many contrasts which give the sparkle to your drawing and fill it with life.

As you render the foliage masses, have in mind the way the leaves radiate from the twigs and branches. While you do not draw in each leaf, your individual strokes will suggest their directions, particularly around the edges. Try as you draw to feel the form of each mass and to model it with variations of tone while keeping its general value in proper key with the whole.

Observe how, on the darker side of the trunk and principal limbs and even in the darkest foliage masses, I have taken into account the reflected light from the ground which helps to express form and adds interest. Your skill in maintaining variety of surface in every part of your sketch while keeping it all in proper relation to the whole will develop with practice, just as mine did. Do not be content with just one or a few trials. Make many. Go outdoors and draw from nature. Compose some trees of your own. Do not forget throughout all this that the proper and frequent sharpening of the pencil is a fundamental preliminary to this particular technique. Success depends upon the clean-cut and precise application of pencil to paper with each stroke calculated to be of maximum expressiveness. An uncontrollable point won't work.

T. KAUTZKY.

LESSON 7—DRAWING THE BIRCH TREE

Just as the oak is strong, rugged, and masculine, the birch, which we will now study, is delicate, graceful, and feminine in its characteristics. I am, of course, thinking of the ordinary white birch seen so frequently in suburban landscapes rather than of the great canoe birch which is found in the virgin forest rising to considerable heights and sometimes having impressive girth. The type of birch I mean grows commonly in clusters — several stems from a single root system. So I have chosen to illustrate a cluster of three in which the trunks, as often occurs, have departed from the straight line of uneventful growth and have acquired that character which comes from a certain amount of struggle for survival in the face of difficulties. Because they have this character they become more interesting to draw and compose more effectively.

We begin, as usual, by blocking out the general forms and masses to establish the proportions of the principal foliage groups and their relation to the slender stems. Two stages of this blocking out process are suggested lightly at the top of the accompanying plate. In the first step, the trees alone are roughly arranged in a group. Carried a little further, the composition is seen to need the addition of a mass of shrubbery behind it to avoid top-heaviness and the foliage of the trees needs to be elaborated a bit and treated in a manner more suggestive of leafiness.

When we have gone this far and have our intentions well in mind we can begin boldly to lay in the values we have decided upon for our composition. The central tree of the group, which is in back of the other two, we determine to make the darkest so as to hold the picture in balance. This decision also enables us to silhouette the trees in front as light against dark, increasing the three dimensional feeling.

Note that the foliage of the birch is thin and tremulous, with lots of openings through which the sky shines and lots of leaves, stirred by the wind, turning their silvery under surfaces to the observer. Many single leaves stand out from the rest, especially around the edges of foliage masses, contributing to the sparkling effect. It should be your aim to express these peculiarities in your sketch. You can do it by using rather short broad strokes, changing their directions all the time and varying their shapes to simulate leaf forms, not too literally but suggestively. Also leave frequent whites.

As with the other trees, the principle of setting light against dark and dark against light is employed to define shapes of stem and branch and leaf mass. This principle holds good even though the bark of the birch trunks and limbs is predominantly white. They will still seem dark against the sky in many places. Where the trunks are silhouetted white against the dark foliage of the shrubbery there will be enough lightness to carry the impression of the light bark throughout the sketch.

In putting tones on the trunks and larger branches it will be well to use short strokes running crosswise rather than longer strokes running lengthwise. Somehow this treatment expresses better the quality of the bark, which has a horizontal grain as is known to every one who has peeled a birch tree. Occasional breaks in the continuity of the shading, leaving white gaps not too long for the eye to carry past, are also in character with this tree. The little section in the upper right-hand corner of the plate will show what I mean.

Be sure to keep the trunks properly slender and tapering delicately all the way to the top. The branches usually tend to curve up from the main stem, particularly near the top of the tree where they are shorter. Lower down they may tend to be more horizontal or to bend down if they have had to carry heavy foliage during the tree's life. Ice storms often permanently change their curvature.

I cannot emphasize too much the importance of the silhouette of foliage masses in conveying the character of a tree. Whether you are conscious of it or not as you look at a specimen you are getting an important part of your impression from the way the edges are broken up against the sky or against other trees or buildings. Try therefore to discern as well as you can what the identifying marks are and give particular care to putting them down in your sketch.

LESSON 8—DRAWING THE ELM TREE

One of the loveliest of our American trees is the elm. Despite the ravages of diseases and parasites and destructive storms, this graceful tree is still found in great numbers distributed through the greater part of this country.

In general form, the skeleton of the elm might be approximately contained within a narrow inverted cone, at least until it nears the top of the tree. Here, its limbs curve out gracefully and continue into the smaller branches which bend down under the weight of the leafage.

The trunk of the elm is substantial. Its lower portion thickens at the base and merges into roots extending downward like great fingers designed to achieve a firm grasp of the soil. Its upper part divides as it begins to spread outward, at a height of perhaps ten to twenty feet above the ground, into continuously tapering limbs. A section through the trunk of the mature tree is commonly not circular but shows bulges which indicate the beginnings of the limbs. These bulges become more pronounced as the point of division is approached, so that they develop naturally into the separate limbs above.

The crown of the tree tends to take the form of an arch, or rather a dome, which is filled out more or less according as the tree has a full, healthy growth or is thinly developed for lack of nourishment or otherwise.

The little sketch in the upper left of the accompanying plate indicates the general envelope of the tree I have taken as my example. This has been more fully developed into the skeleton and foliage masses as seen at the upper right. As with the other trees we have studied, we begin our sketch thus by establishing its essentials.

In the sketch fully developed on the plate, it will be noted that I have used both types of stroke in modeling the trunk, limbs, and branches. Some of the strokes are curved to suggest the form of the limbs and define the shadows falling across them. As in the preceding lessons, where the limbs or branches occur against a background of foliage, they are left white. Where they are seen against the sky they are dark in shadow, gray in light.

In expressing the foliage, short, broad strokes, slightly curving and following the general direction of the arching sweep of the tree's crown, are applied with values already decided upon in accordance with the way the light falls. The portions of the foliage receiving most intense light may be completely highlighted, suggested only by a few strokes around their edges or by silhouetting them against darker masses. Portions receiving normal light will be shown by various degrees of gray. Keep plenty of variety in these gray areas and allow bits of white to show through here and there. Watch the silhouettes of the edges of each group of leaves so that they will be suggestive of the way the leaves hang down. It may be well at this point to turn back and compare this tree with the oak shown in Lesson 6. You can see by comparing the two plates, better than I can tell you in words, the difference in character of the strokes used. While the individual strokes do not stand out too prominently, they count enough to give direction to the leaf arrangement and differentiate one type of tree from the other so far as that feature is concerned.

One of the things you must always have in mind, just as in drawing other subjects, is the matter of proper proportioning. The weight of the trunk and limbs of each kind of tree bears a characteristic relationship to the whole tree. I mention this because I often encounter drawings of elm trees where the trunks are too thin in proportion to the rest. Note the apparent swelling in the size of the trunk where it merges into the limbs and also the merging of the trunk into the principal roots at the point of contact with the ground. When you once see these things you will never thereafter be guilty of drawing elms that seem to have smooth cylindrical trunks, resting on the ground like up-ended pipes and branching abruptly into smaller pipes.

Now please do not immediately undertake to prove me wrong by bringing up examples of elm trees which do not conform to the general statements I have made. There are exceptions in nature to almost every rule, but what we are trying to do here is to learn how to draw trees which satisfy the artistic eye yet are natural.

LESSON 9—MORE ON ROOF TEXTURES

Having learned something about drawing trees, upon which we have been concentrating for the last four lessons, let us turn again to the problem of indicating the textures of architectural materials. For this lesson I have chosen as examples two different types of roof—one of tile, old and weatherbeaten, and the other of slate, new but pleasantly irregular of surface.

Recall that in Lesson 4 we decided that the shingled roof required three principal directions of pencil strokes — parallel to the grain of the wood, parallel to the shingle courses, and parallel to the direction of light. The same general rule may be applied here. The difference between the rough and the smooth texture is achieved by the greater or less degree of irregularity of the individual strokes, not by their general directions. The irregularity of the strokes is to be found in their departure from both straightness and uniformity of tone.

The quality of any texture can be best rendered by one who comprehends how that texture came into being. This means knowing not only how the individual units are put together and supported to form, for example, a roof, but also the characteristics of these units — shingles, shakes, tiles, slates or whatnot—and, most important, the things that happen to such surfaces by the action of nature over a period of time.

Rain, falling upon a sloping roof and running down its length, streaks it with dirt washed from the sky or previously deposited by the wind. Melting snow does likewise. Alternate wetting and drying, heat and cold, affect soft materials like wood while leaving harder substances like slate or terra cotta essentially unchanged in form. Shingles and shakes become furrowed as the softer part of their grain is eroded away and also tend to curl up at the edges instead of lying permanently flat. Sagging between rafters tends to develop with age in wood construction, producing a more or less perceptible waviness across a roof that has yielded again and again to snow loads and wind pressure. Wind-blown seeds and spores find lodging in the crevices of a roughly textured roof and some of them develop into mosses and lichens if conditions are favorable. Shingles or slates become loosened in old roofs and slip out of place or even blow completely away. All of these things and many more enter into the development of a roof texture. Understanding them, you will be better able to draw convincingly. Imagination, the ability to see beyond the obvious, to penetrate with your mind below the surface of things, is necessary if you are to be an artist. But we degress, perhaps!

The examples shown here illustrate many of the things I have dwelt on during all the preceding lessons. Must I really point them out to you? The cleanly-defined broad strokes with few dominant directions; the gradation of tones; the contrasts of light against dark, dark against light; the avoidance of monotony; the sparkling little flecks of white paper showing through; the carefully considered silhouette: you can surely see them. And what I can do, you can do — if you will only *work*, and THINK!

It is all right, if you wish, to copy these sketches, just to get the feeling of the different type of strokes and to develop capacity to produce deep darks and delicate lights simply by varying the pressure of pencil on paper as described in Lesson 1. More important to you, however, is the making of many sketches of your own, working direct from nature if possible. You will find many textures not illustrated here and it is your job to express them as well as you can. The same fundamental strokes can be used for all of them, the general principle of this particular technique being to use broad strokes, for the sake of economy of effort, wherever possible. Narrow strokes may be used, where your intelligence directs, for definition or accents. You will find plenty of places in the sketches in this series where I have used narrow strokes but I do not believe you will find any where broad strokes would have done the work. I mention this simply because I have frequently encountered the type of student mind that delights in pointing out instances where the teacher has apparently disregarded his own instructions. Rules, of course, are made to be broken but it requires experience to know exactly when to break them.

LESSON 10—EVERGREEN SHRUBBERY

Dark accents in the landscape settings for architecture are frequently furnished by shrubs and hedges of yew, box, and other hardy evergreens. Sometimes these are clipped and sometimes they are left to take their natural forms but in any case they constitute a special problem for the artist or delineator. Their close, compact growth and their dark tones make them conspicuous elements in the picture in which they occur. They must therefore be drawn with care and sufficient naturalness.

The sketch at the top of the accompanying plate shows a suburban house of common enough type with a setting of rather formal planting. The most prominent features of this landscape are a thick box hedge in the foreground and some clipped evergreen tree forms which might well be English yew, or perhaps cedar. Nearer to the house is a hedge with an evergreen arch framing the garden gate. The dark values of these elements outweigh any other dark tone in the composition. To render them properly will call for heavy pressure with your 4B pencil properly sharpened to produce clean broad strokes.

As a preliminary to tackling the problem presented by this sketch or one of your own composition involving similar elements, I advise (as I have done before) that you go outdoors and look at some actual samples of box, yew, cedar, and other evergreens. Observe the bubbling forms of the box, its texture, the way the light falling upon it models its shape and reflects from the portions in full sunlight, making almost highlights. Notice in the cedars how there are occasional gaps in the otherwise close growth, through which you can see bits of branch, or even the sky. Mark particularly the silhouette, whether or not the specimen is clipped, standing with more or less irregularity against lighter areas beyond. See how the contrast of dark against light gives the illusion of an aura extending along the line of separation. Get all these impressions firmly in your mind and then come in and go to work.

In drawing the box hedge shown on the facing page, I have used several types of broad strokes, which have, however, but two general purposes.

One group of strokes serves to define and model the general forms while the other is directed to the expression of texture. The former are rather long, curving strokes, sometimes wavy, and they follow the contours of the bushes quite clearly. Their variations in tone are calculated to indicate the play of direct and reflected light across the interlacement of globular surfaces which characterize this plant. The other set of strokes are short and multi-directional. They may be seen most distinctly on the nearest bush at the left. The suggestion of leafage which these convey is strong enough to carry the impression through the whole length of the hedge, especially when reinforced by the wavy or zig-zaggy strokes of the first category. I have let the white paper show through here and there to express the highlights that occur where the sun reflects from the shiny foliage at the proper angle. Note that, though the general tone of the whole is dark, there is plenty of variety, as there would be in nature. Even in the blackest shadows the density is not complete.

The tall, clipped trees are modeled as cylinders, with reflected light bringing out the roundness of the shadow side. Here, too, I have used a number of short strokes running in many different directions and also have taken particular pains to accent and properly portray the irregular silhouette. The same remarks apply to the hedge and gate beyond. Note throughout the sketch that I have left a thin though irregular strip of white paper along the top and lighted sides of these evergreen forms. This helps the general sunny effect and accords with truth.

The hedge at the bottom of the plate is intended to be privet, which may not be, strictly speaking, an evergreen. It is rendered with a great many short strokes, laid closely in all directions. I have been careful to define the silhouette in character with the plant and have left a number of irregular openings in the foliage through which some of the stems and twigs may be seen. This makes a more interesting and none the less truthful picture than if I had assumed a solid growth of leaves. Longer diagonal strokes, following the direction of light, were used for the shadows.

LESSON 11—INDICATING FLOWERS

Occasionally, when sketching garden scenes or bits of architecture, it becomes necessary to include some flower groupings or borders. It is therefore a good idea to be prepared to handle this special problem. The problem becomes easy if you remember one simple principle—*it is the silhouette that counts most.* I am of course thinking in terms of sketches at relatively small scale and not of close-up, still life studies of flowers where more detail is called for. But even in the latter case the silhouette is always very important.

The two sketches on the accompanying plate illustrate the principle as applied to small and medium scale representation. The little garden pool and fountain above is set off to advantage against a bit of clipped hedge which also serves to make the flowers seen more effectively. This principle of placing flower beds where they will have a background of dark foliage is well known to garden designers and you can find innumerable instances of such treatment, both formal and informal. The advantage it gives to your sketch is obvious. By making the hedge suitably dark and letting the flowers stand out against it, a sparkling result is accomplished, almost colorful in its effect. It will be noted that it is entirely unnecessary to draw or indicate individual petals. The shape of the flower as seen silhouetted against the dark hedge is sufficient identification, taken together with its leaves and stems, to permit you to be just as literal as you wish. A little study of different species of flower plants will give you a working repertoire of forms that will equip you for sketching any garden you are likely to encounter in reality or in imagination. Where the dark background is not present, as for example to the right and left of the hedge in my sketch, the silhouetting is done in reverse — dark against light. Different degrees of gray will suggest different hues for the blossoms.

At the bottom of the plate I have drawn, at somewhat larger scale, some flowers planted against the base of a house. The house is light in color, but open windows provide some dark areas against which a few blossoms stand out clearly. The shadows cast by the plant foliage also make dark areas along the bottom of the wall which cause the sunlit leaves to stand out sharply. Your problem is thus to define the various shapes plausibly, in accordance with your observation and knowledge, blending the contrast of dark against light and light against dark so that the observer will not be conscious of where one type of contrast leaves off and the other begins. As usual, the greatest degree of contrast will be at the center of interest with softer contrasts towards the edges.

You have by this time been drilled enough in the application of broad strokes, long and short, straight and curved, so that I do not feel that it is necessary to go through an analysis of this plate from that point of view. As always, it is necessary to keep your pencil well and frequently sharpened and to exercise all the control of which you are capable over each individual stroke. So far as you fall short of complete control your sketches will be fuzzy and will lack that crispness for which, I presume, you are striving.

This is as good a place as any to encourage the exercise of freedom in composition, tempered with understanding of what you are doing. If you are sketching from nature, you do not need to adhere literally to what you see before you. You may move trees or bushes or rocks about to fit the needs of your picture, provided of course you do not place them in some impossible position. You can exaggerate the slope of a hill or suppress it, all within the bounds of common sense. Such things as architecture you had perhaps best take as they are, unless you are an architectural designer who knows why and how things are put together. Even with buildings, however, you have some latitude — in the handling of shadows cast upon them, for example. In drawing trees, you can take liberties with the placing of branches, so long as you are true to species, or you may omit portions of the foliage if by so doing you make a more pleasing composition. In short, by using your brains you can be the master of your picture instead of letting it master you. Until you have acquired this mastery, you cannot fairly be described as an artist.

LESSON 12—COMPOSITION POINTERS

We now come to what is perhaps the most diffi-cult thing for the young artist to grasp — the baffling subject of Composition. It is not a mat-ter of rules, though there are certain guiding principles that are generally taught and which are helpful. They are to be found in many books. In the end, however, the quality of the results obtained springs from some inborn artis-tic sense which you either have or do not have. The real artist must have it. With it, he fre-quently defies the rules or laws or whatever you may call them, and produces masterpieces of ar-rangement that could never have been arrived at by conformation to any established standards. Yet it is not for beginners to set out to break precedent and for that reason they had best acknowledge certain principles that experience has found generally reliable. A few of these are illustrated by the little pairs of sketches shown opposite. Since I omitted to number these on the drawing, let us agree to refer to them in discus-sion as 1, 2, 3, 4, and 5, reading from the top down. Faults occur in the left-hand column and are to be seen corrected, in a simplified way, in the right-hand column.

Sketch number 1, in its initial form, is too strongly dominated by horizontals and also lacks a definite center of interest. It needs some verti-cal accents to break up the monotonous hori-zontal movement and also will benefit by in-creasing the contrasts near the doorway and tapering off their strength to the right and left. By introducing a tree or two rising from behind the building we can achieve the required vertical contrast, carefully avoiding stiff symmetry by balancing foliage masses of different size around our chosen axis rather than centering one upon it. The horizontality is further reduced by changing the direction of the shadow strokes across the foreground. The rearrangement of contrast in value is obvious; its effect unde-niably beneficial.

Number 2 shows a view down a road with all the perspective lines converging to a point far at the left. The result is unsatisfying because the eye is constantly being pulled out of the picture. We must insert some elements to stop this wan-dering of attention and hold it near the center of the picture where it belongs. So we strike in a telegraph pole which furnishes a strong barrier across the eye-compelling convergencies, placing it where it will define the left-hand limit of the central area of interest. Because a vertical pole alone would be stiff and uninteresting, we tilt it a little, give it some supports, and let some poi-son ivy soften its otherwise hard profile. We also put in a background tree behind the row of houses. Its position keeps the pole from jutting too prominently into the sky and it also helps to direct the eye back to the center of interest which we now emphasize with increased detail and contrasting values. A suggestion of grass and weeds along the edge of the road, accented with a shadow from the pole, join with a few strokes laid across the road to keep the attention from wandering out at the lower right.

The third sketch suffers from too strong con-trasts at the left side, the relatively unimportant tree getting all the attention. The house, after all, is the most interesting element here. By re-arranging the values as shown, better balance around the center is achieved and the house now stands out clearly. The dark tree compensates for the dark gable end. The tree at the left is still there but is well grayed down and the dark shrubbery has been wisely eliminated.

In sketch number 4 a garage has been added to the same general group used in 3. The first try resulted in giving this garage as much attention as the house. As revised, attention has been brought back to the house by changing the di-rection of light, redistributing the values, intro-ducing some dark foliage at strategic points, and using the direction of shadow lines to carry the eye where it is wanted. See if you cannot follow the process through and discover the reason be-hind each change. Then recompose the whole group in a different way. The last pair of sketches merely calls attention to the improve-ment that may be made in a "two value" compo-sition by adding a middle tone. The grays give the forms more solidity and hold the whole thing together. This would be even more evi-dent if the drawing were made at larger scale.

PART II
PORTFOLIO OF BROAD STROKE DRAWINGS

FORT TRYON PARK, NEW YORK

WEST VIEW FROM PARK DRIVE
FORT TRYON PARK, MANHATTAN

THEO KAUTZKY

CATHEDRAL, COUTANCES, NORMANDY

VIEW AT GAVARNIE, PYRENEES

VIEW TOWARD GAVARNIE, PYRENEES

STREET, ROCKPORT, MASSACHUSETTS

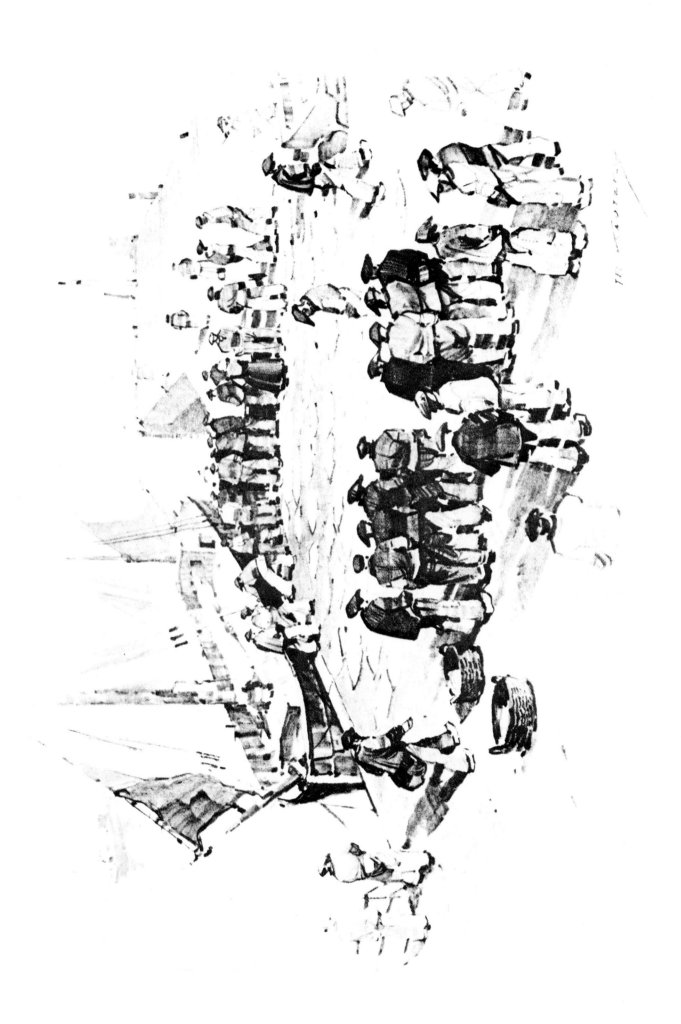

HARBOR, CAMARET, BRITTANY

CHURCH, IRVINGTON-ON-HUDSON, NEW YORK

AERIAL RENDERING

STREET, LANNION, BRITTANY

STREET, CHARLESTON, SOUTH CAROLINA

TED KAUTZKY

FISHING BOAT, DOUARNENEZ, BRITTANY

SHRINE, TREGASTEL, BRITTANY

BEACH, TREGASTEL, BRITTANY

STONE HOUSE, MAINE

CHAPEL, LANDEMER, NORMANDY

FISHERMEN, MORGAT, BRITTANY

RENDERING OF FIELDSTON BRIDGE, NEW YORK

Henry Hudson Parkway
Fieldston Bridge

63